Vol 10

MAZE

Ages 4-6

FOR KIDS

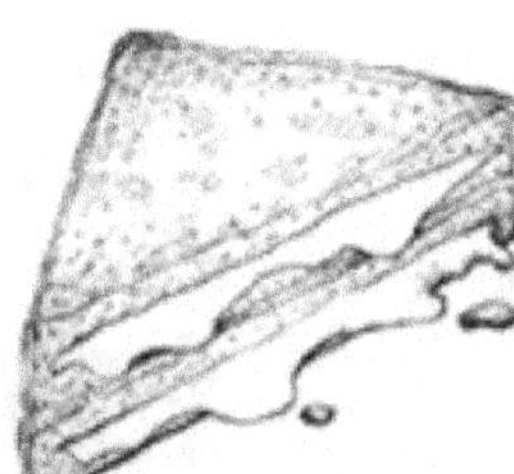

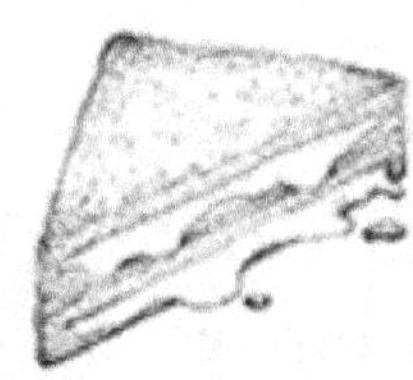

MAZE BOOK

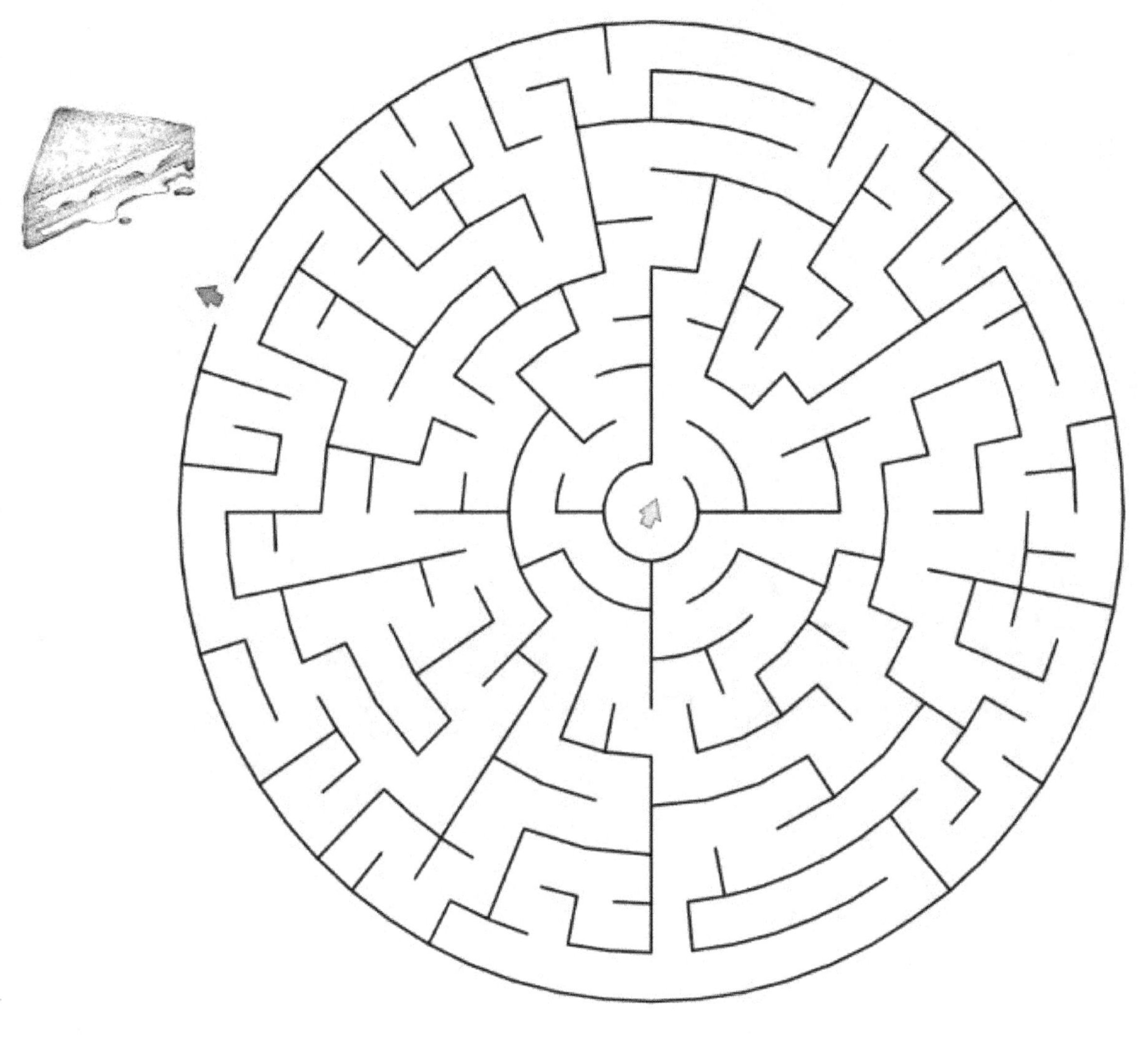

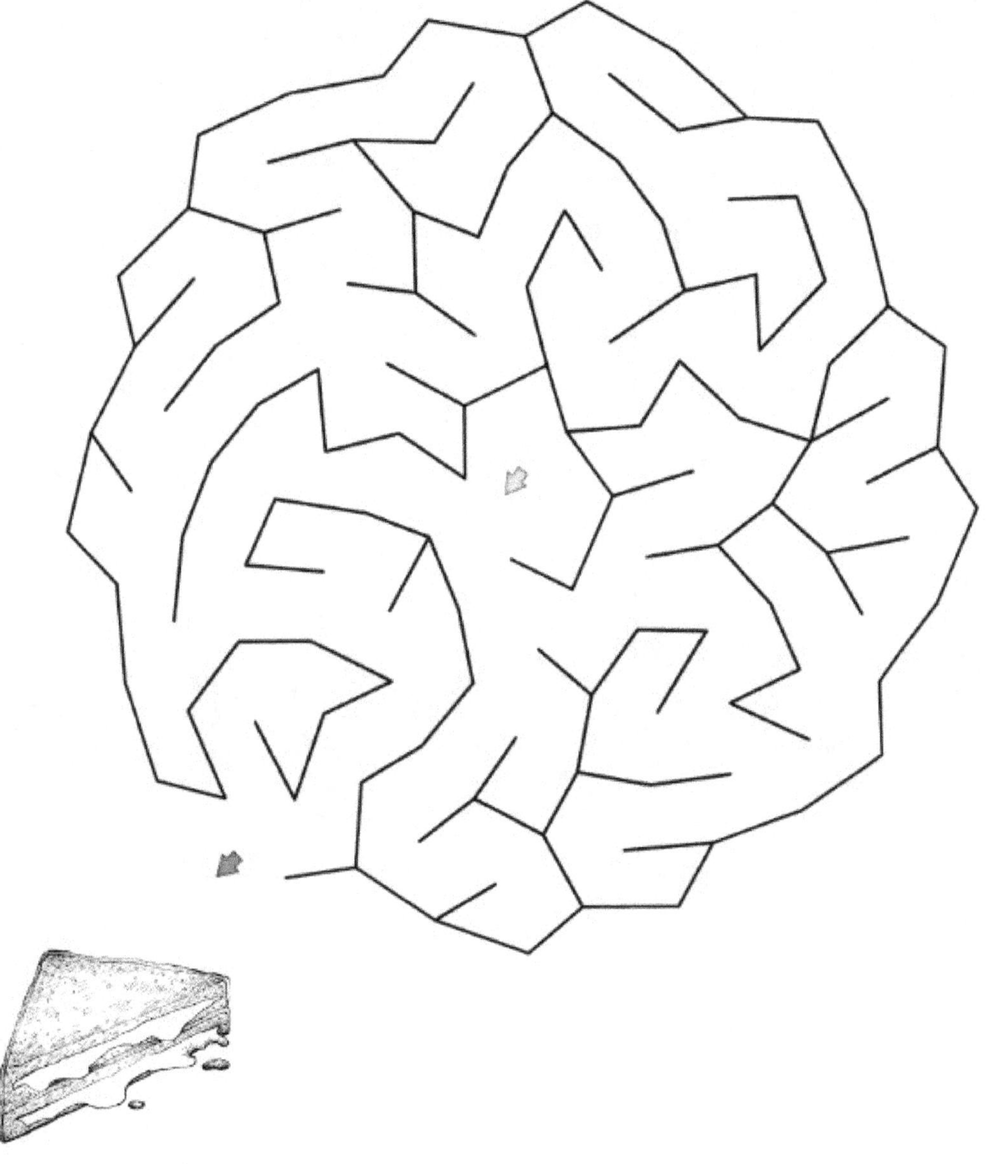

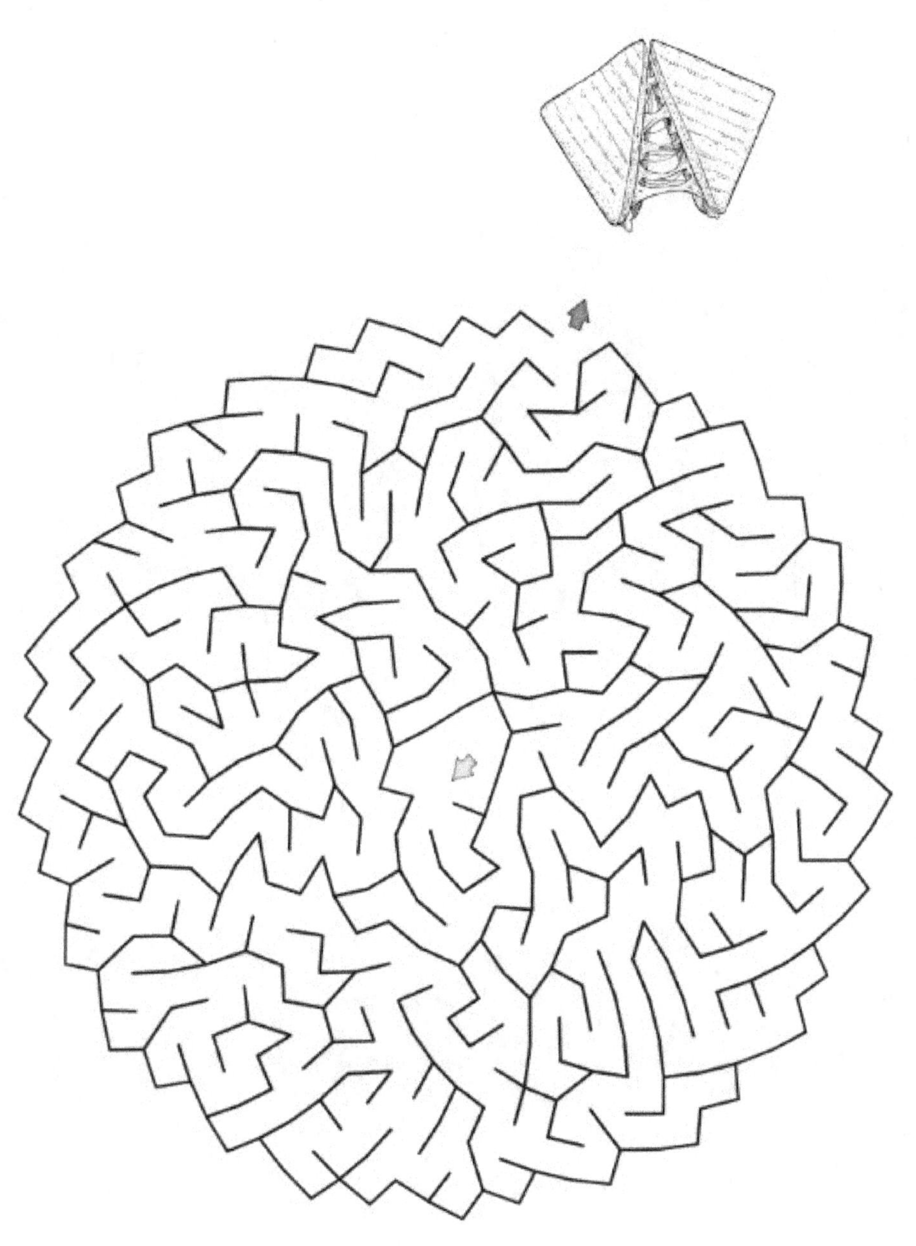

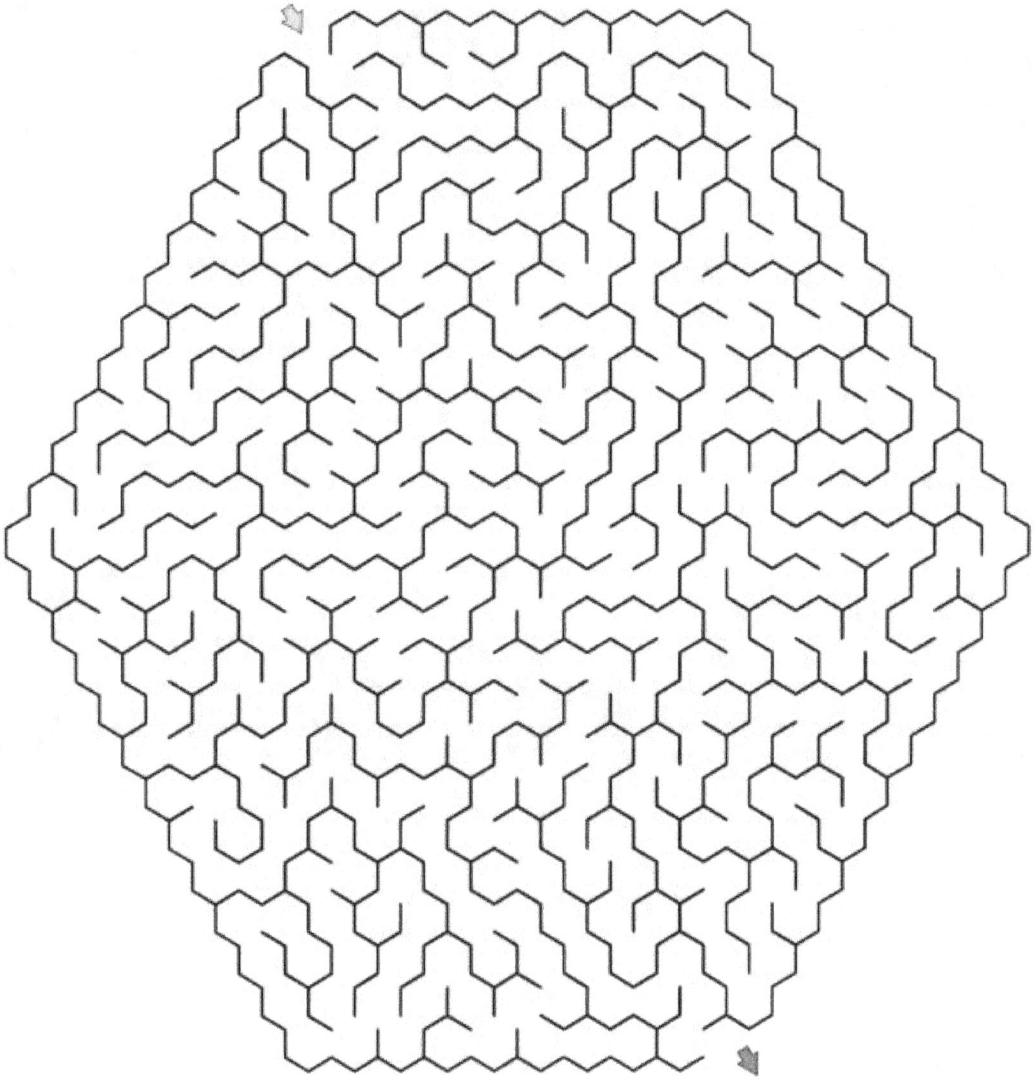

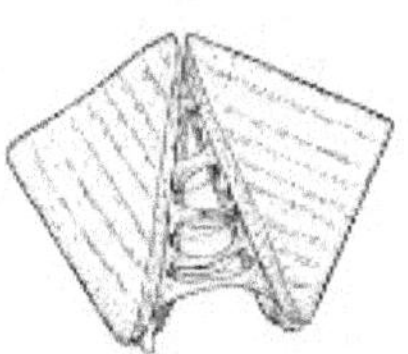

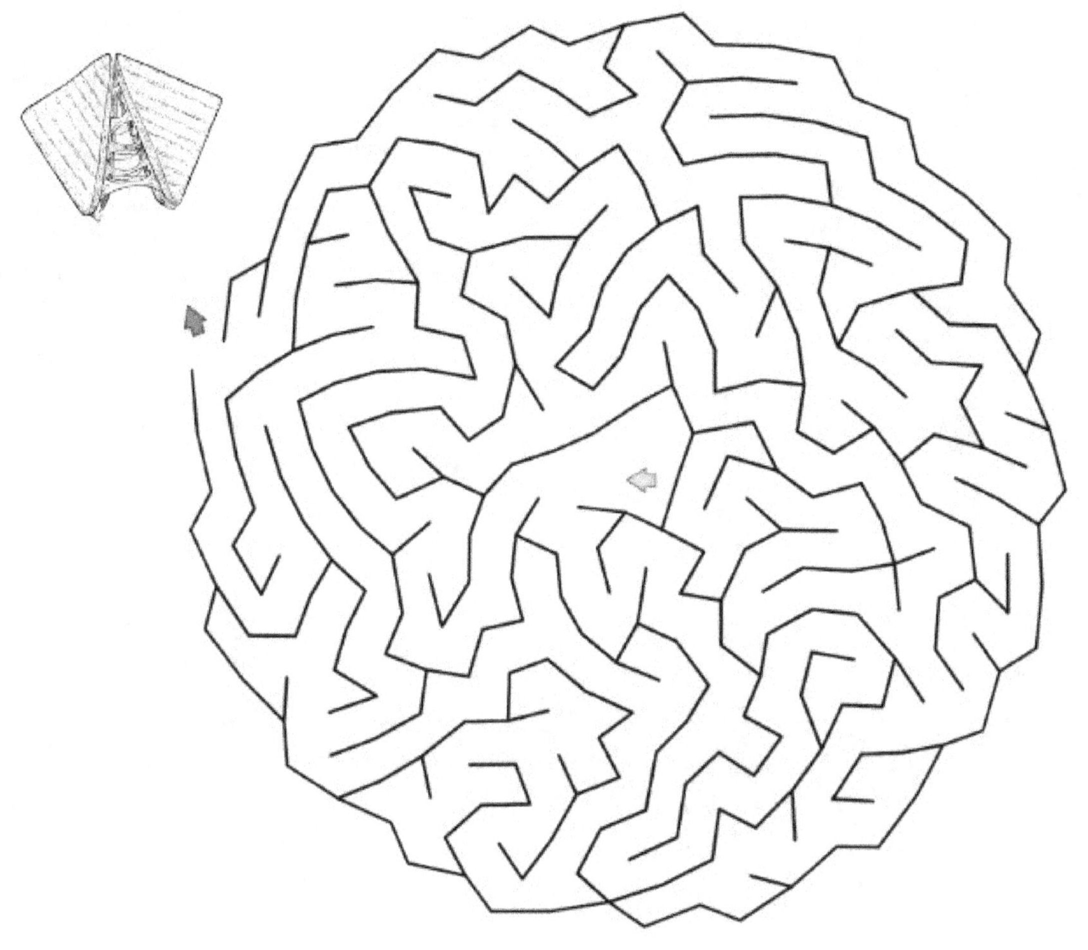

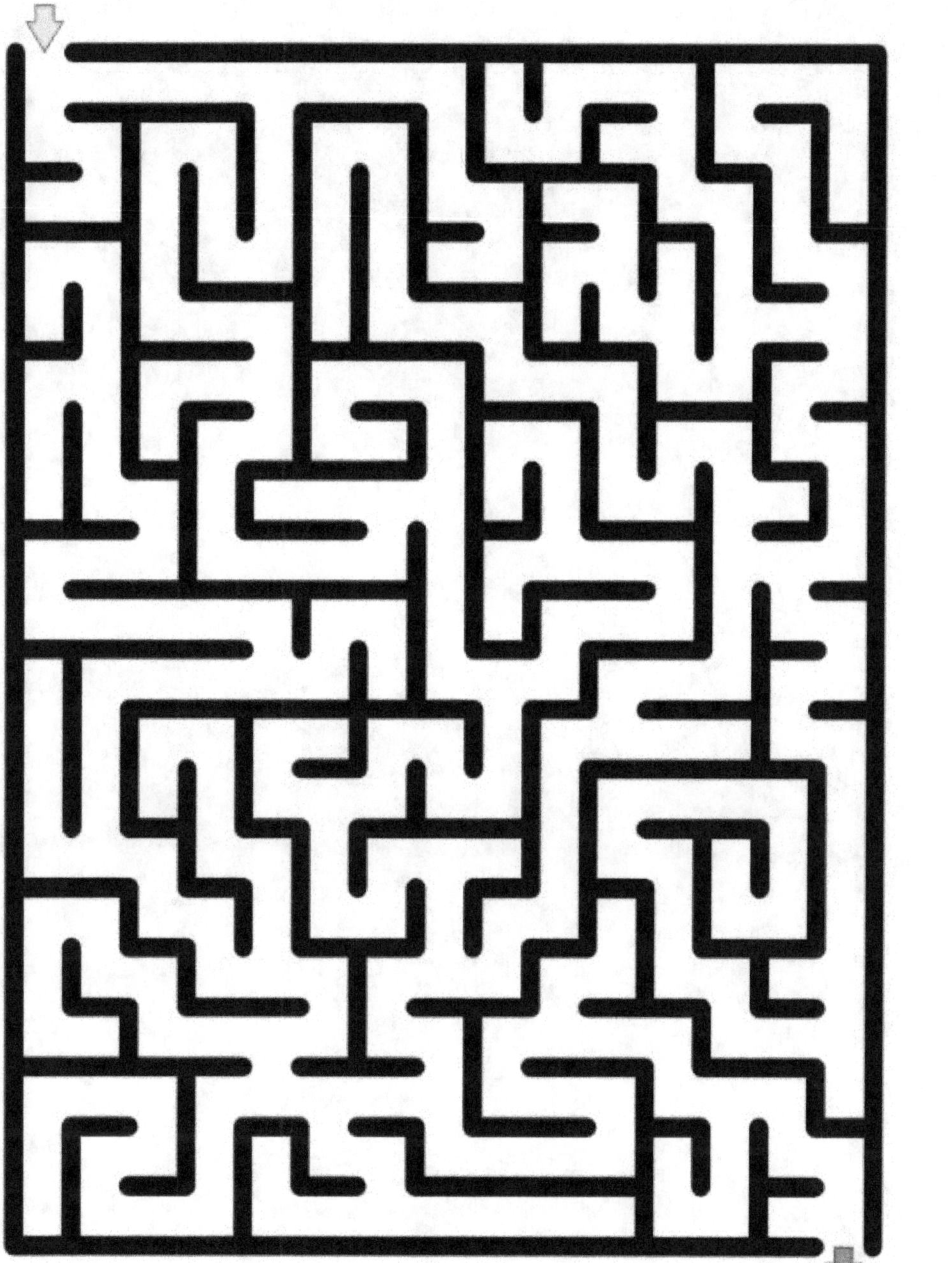

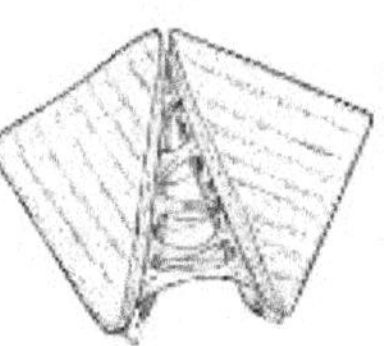

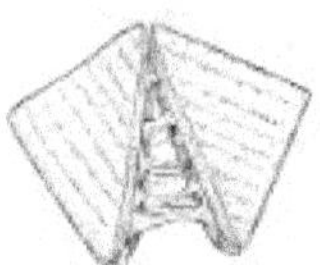

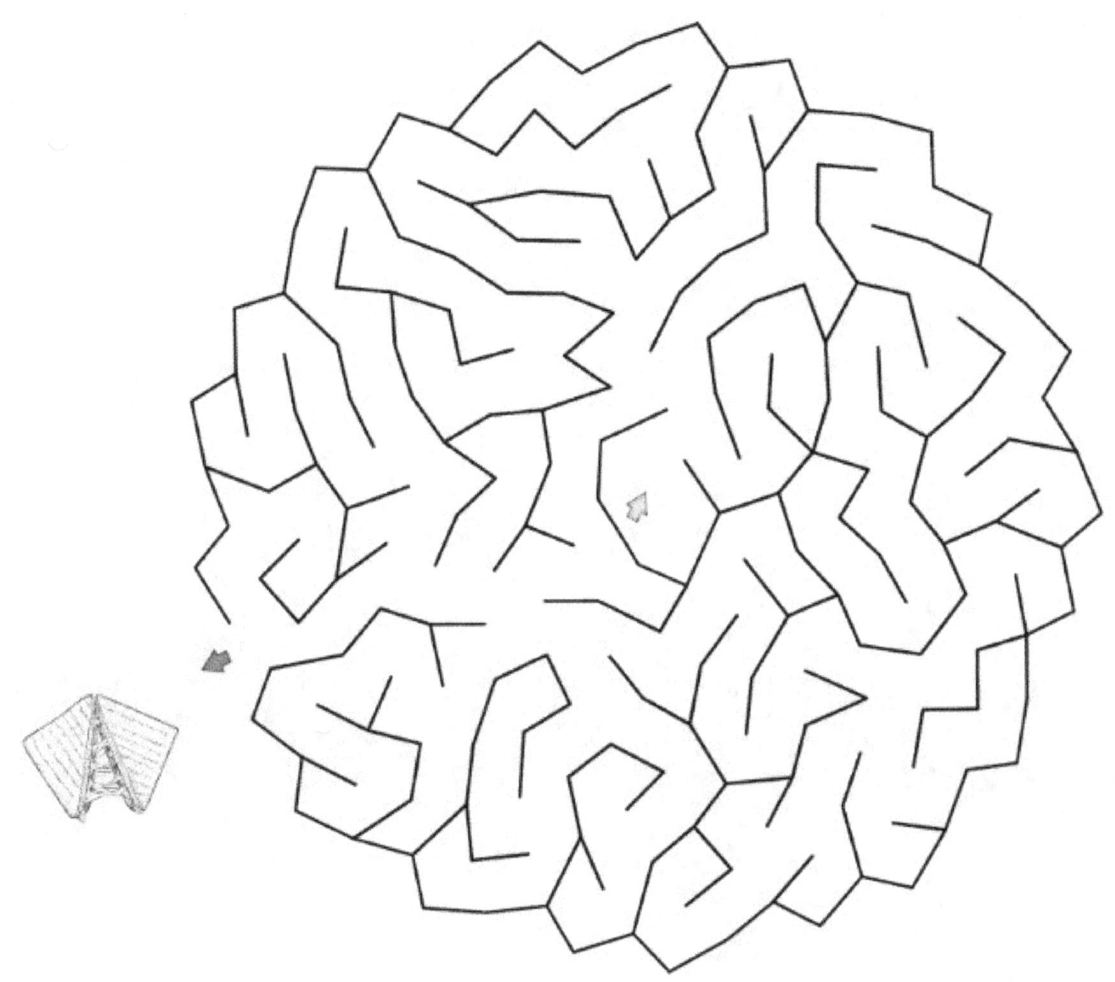
A

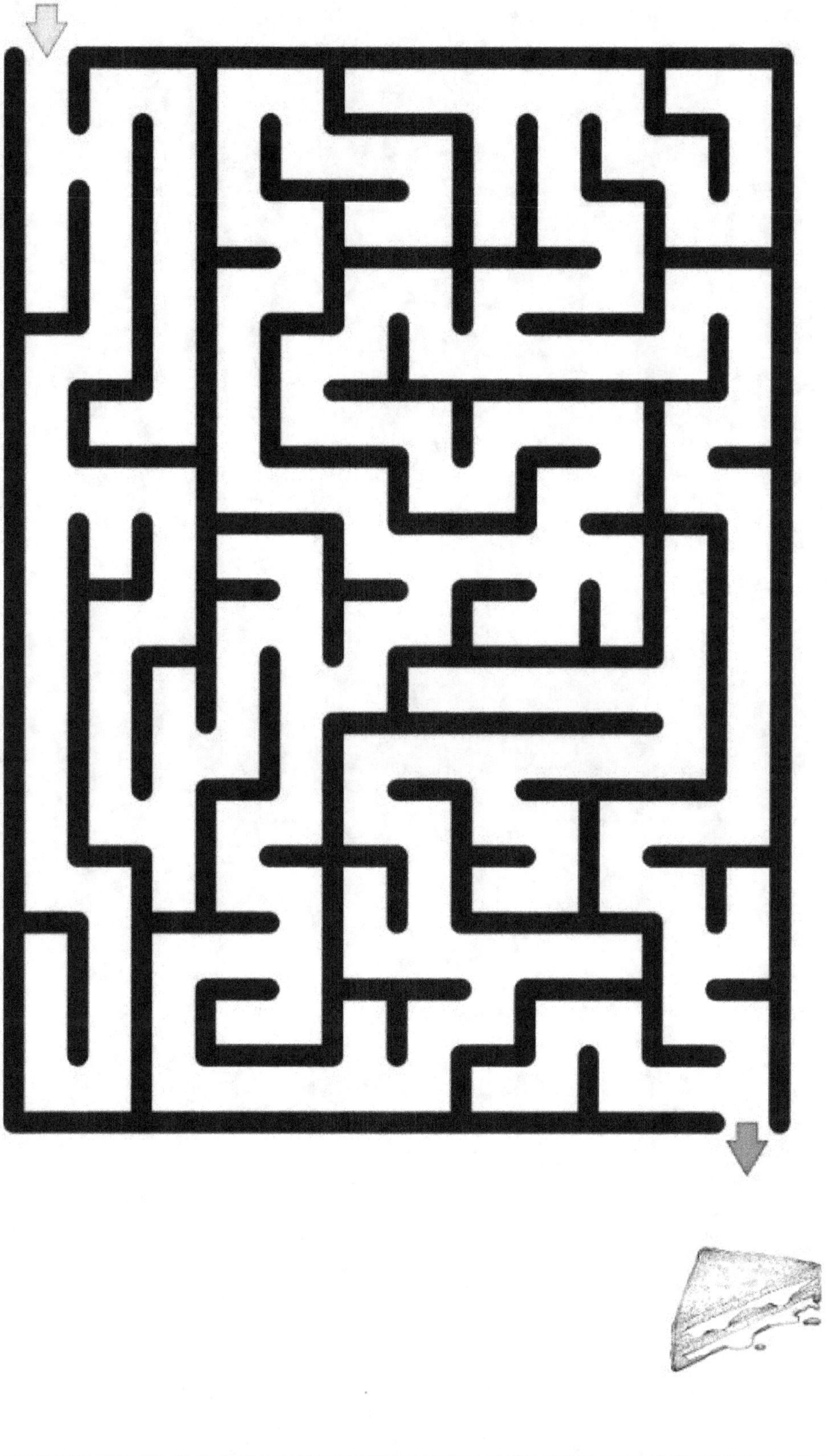

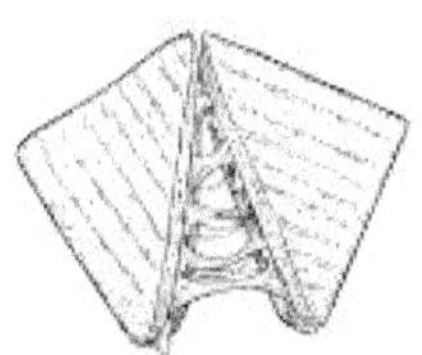

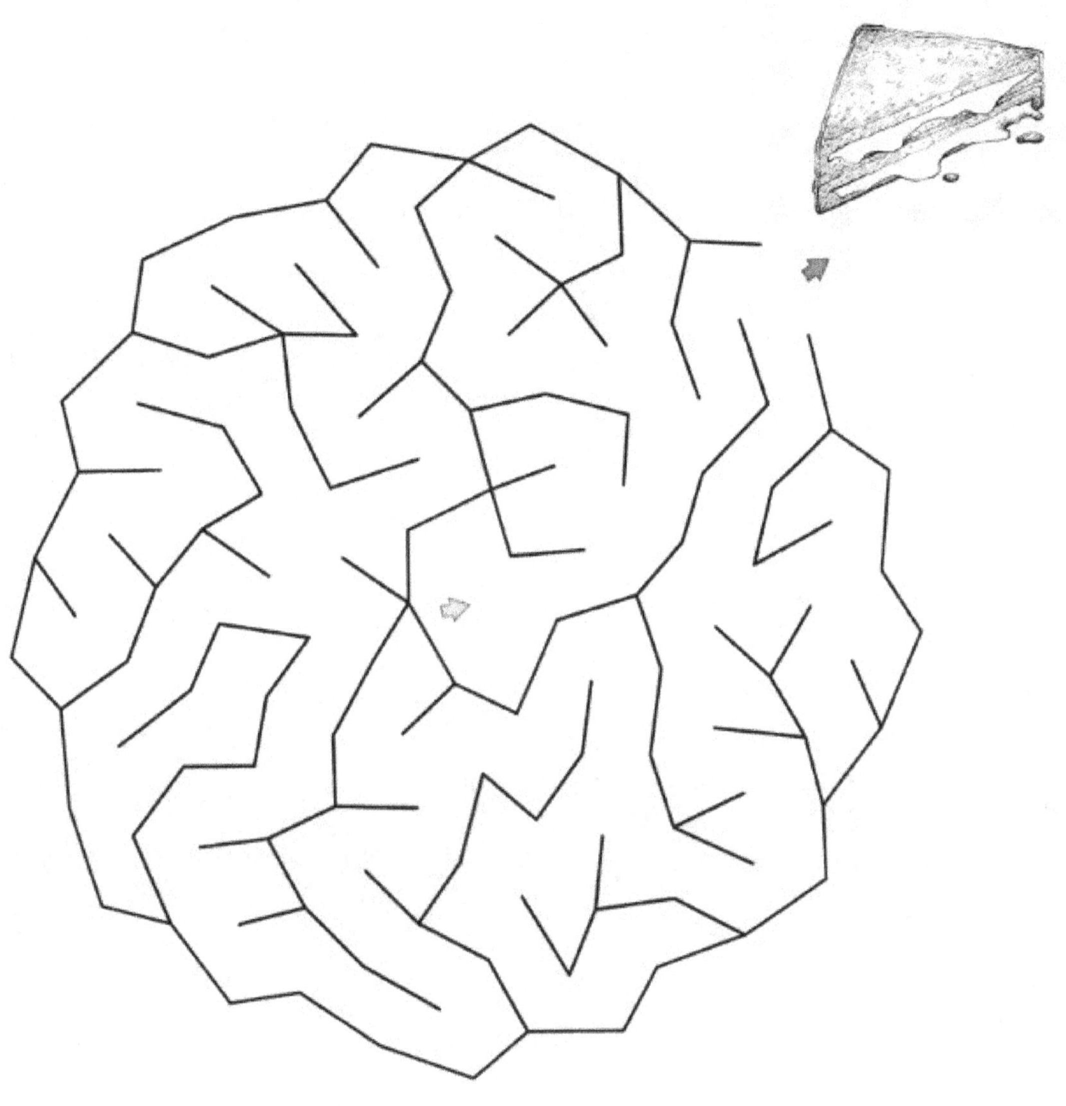

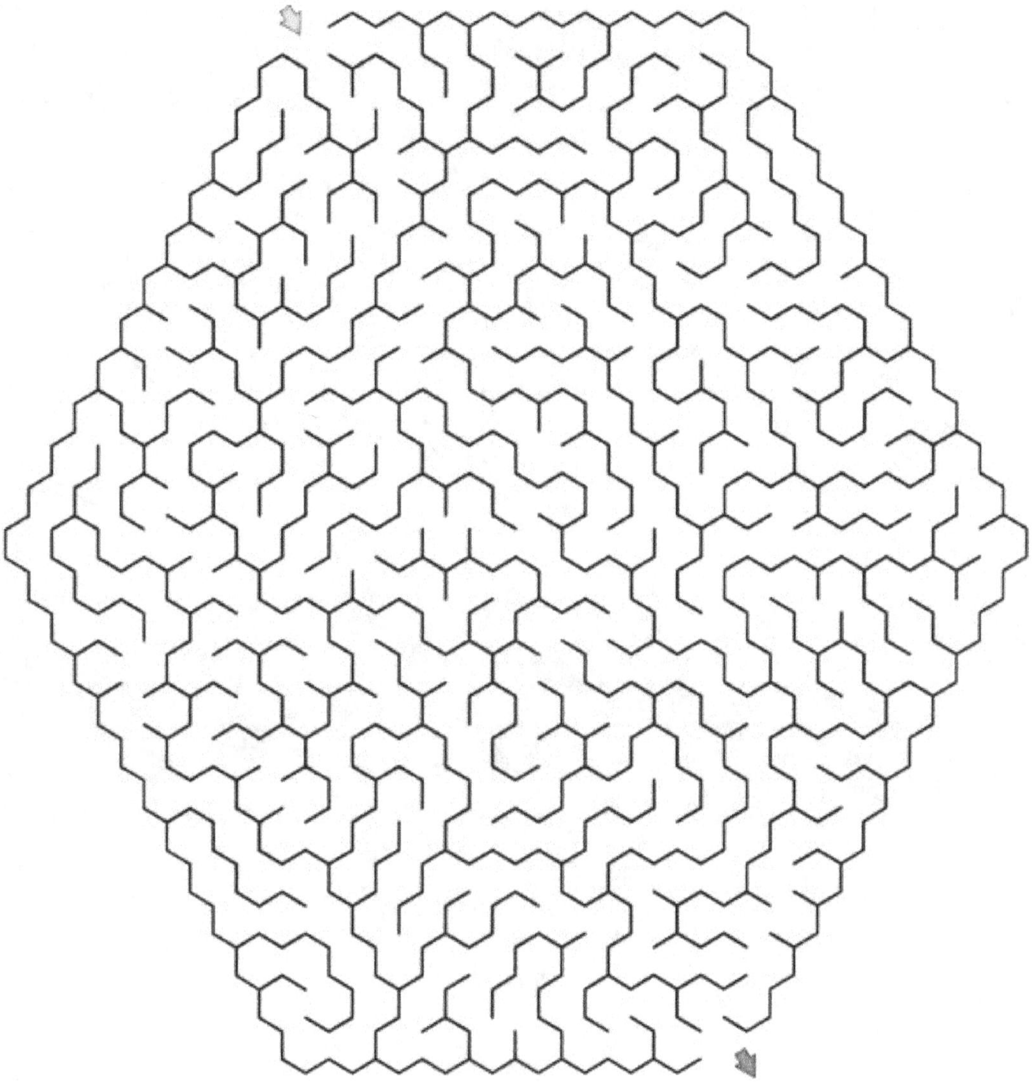

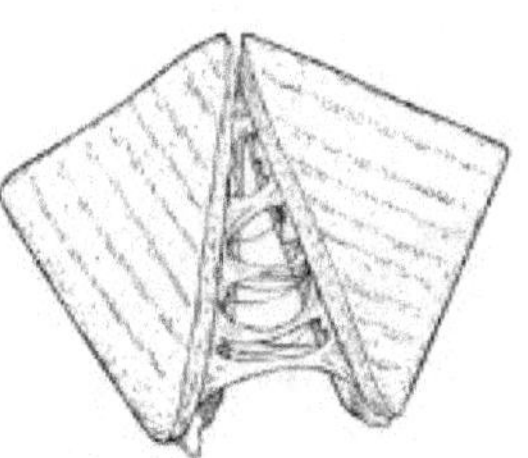

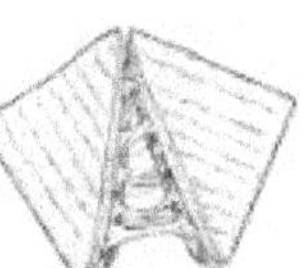

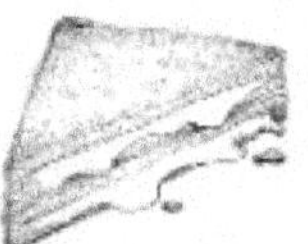

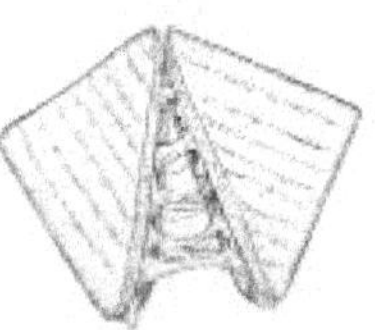

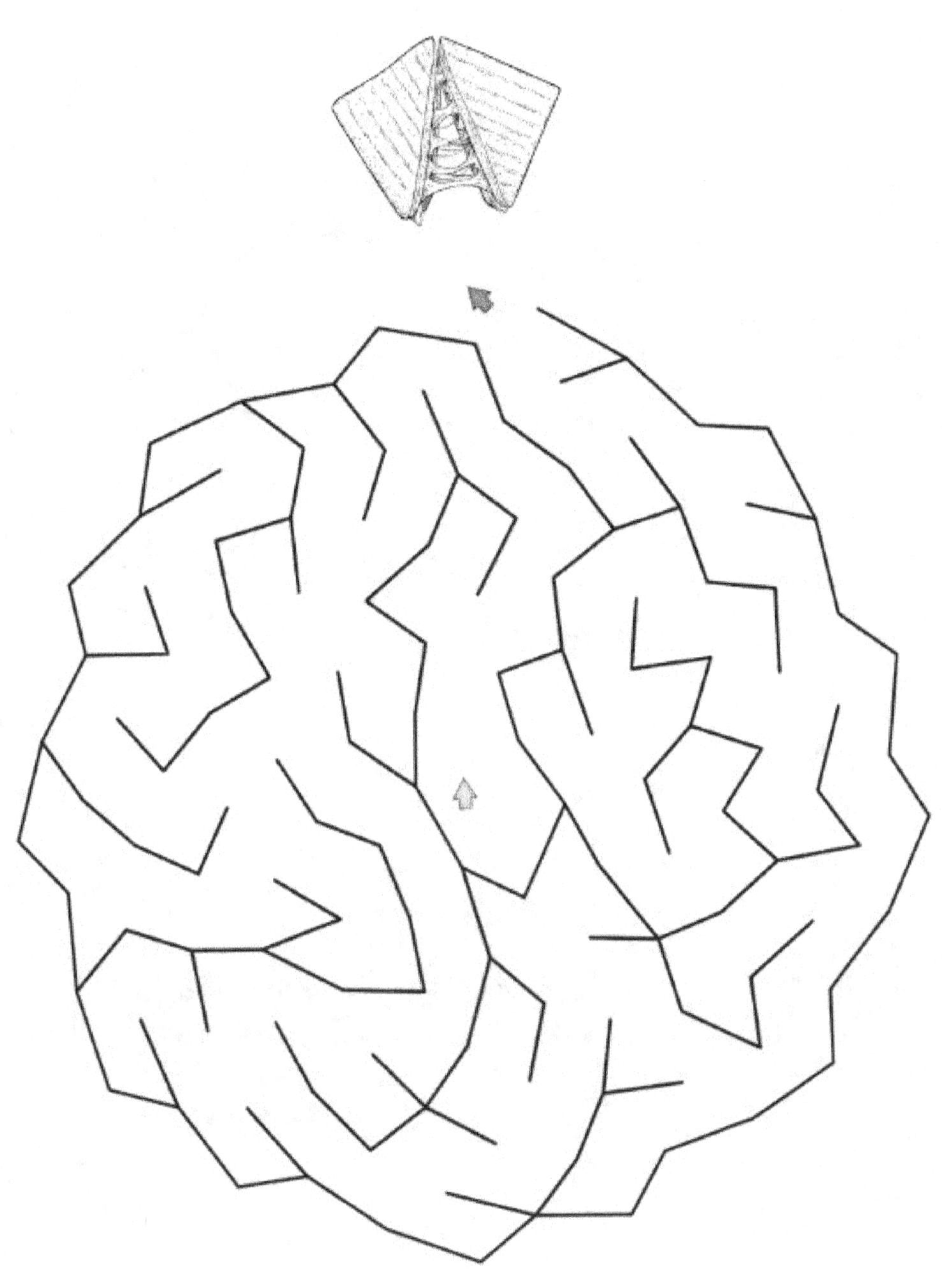

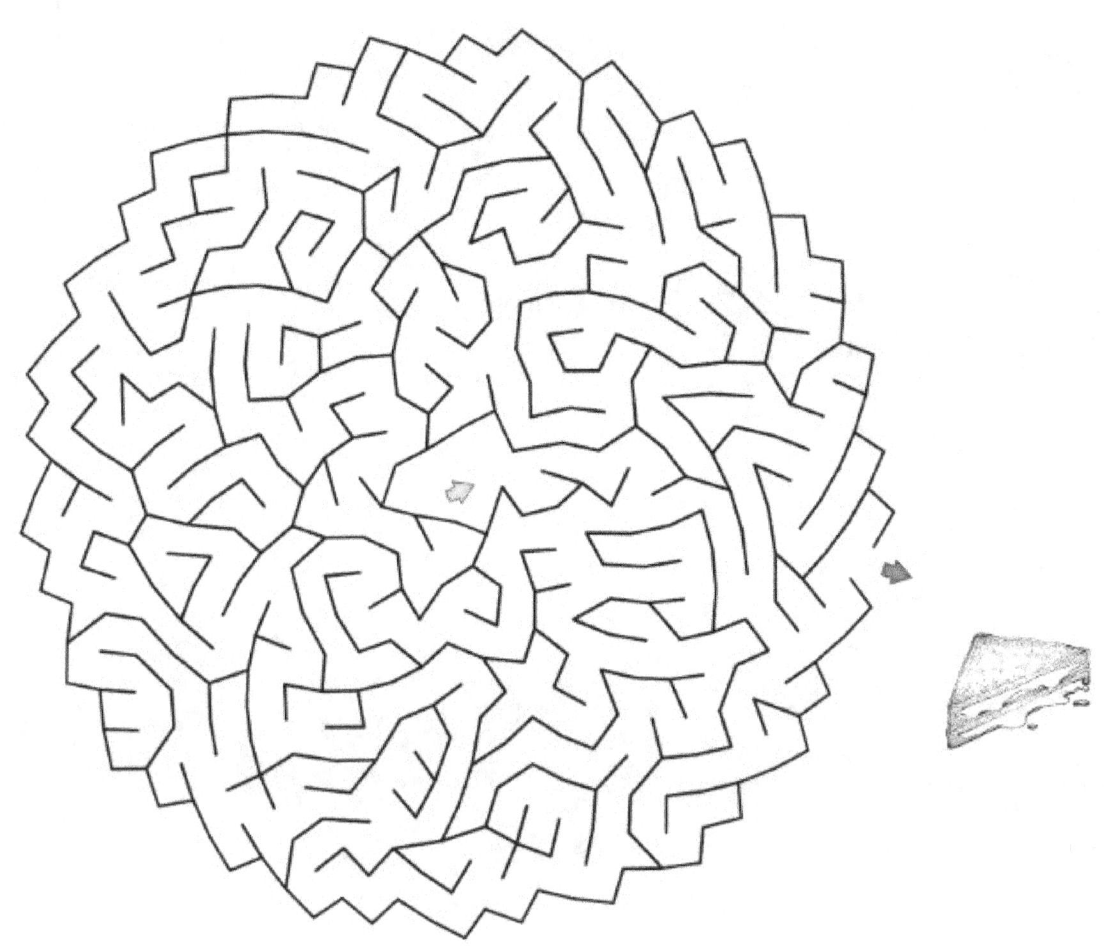

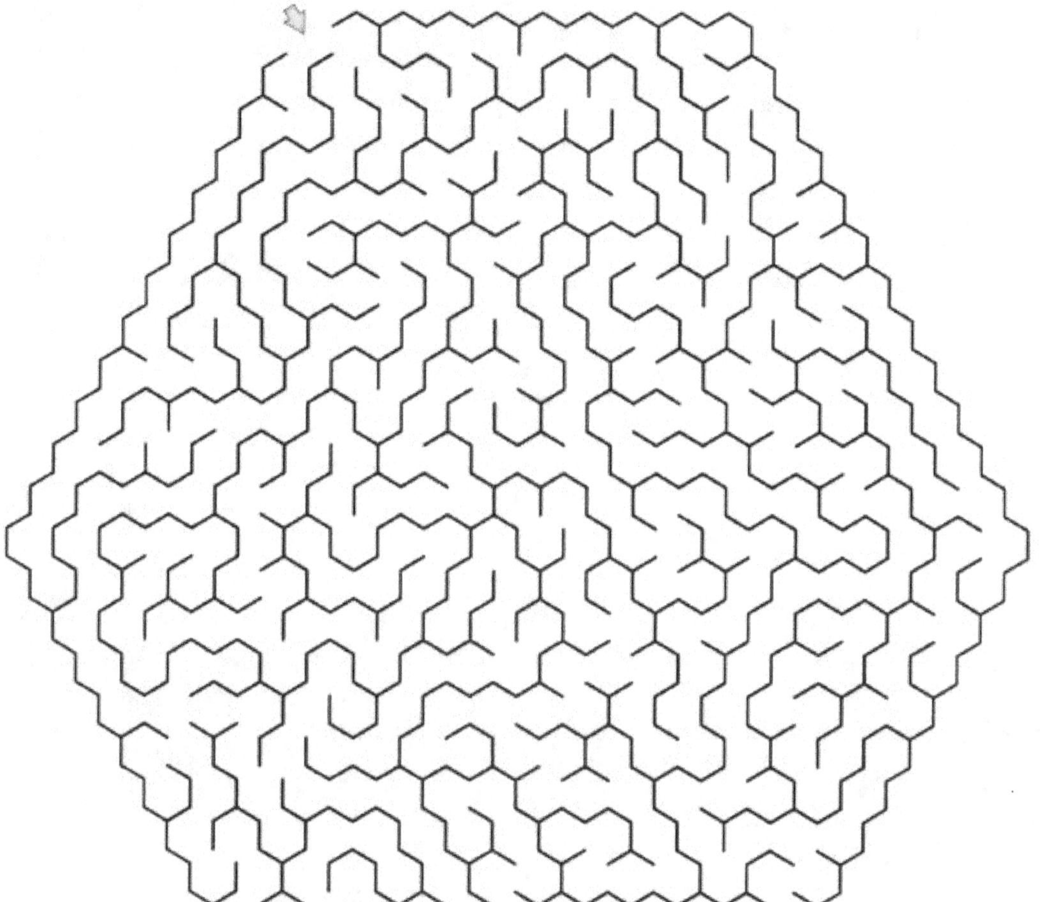

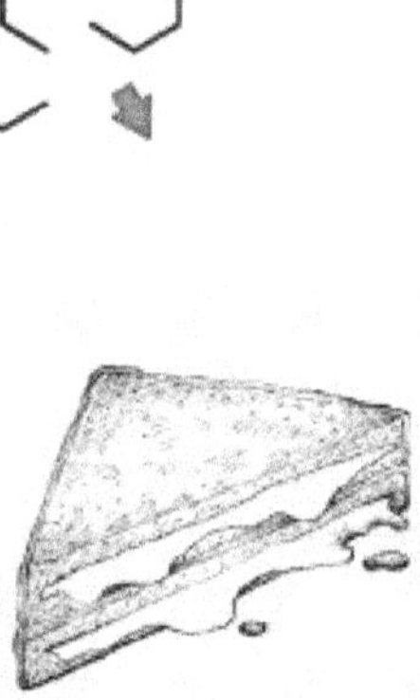

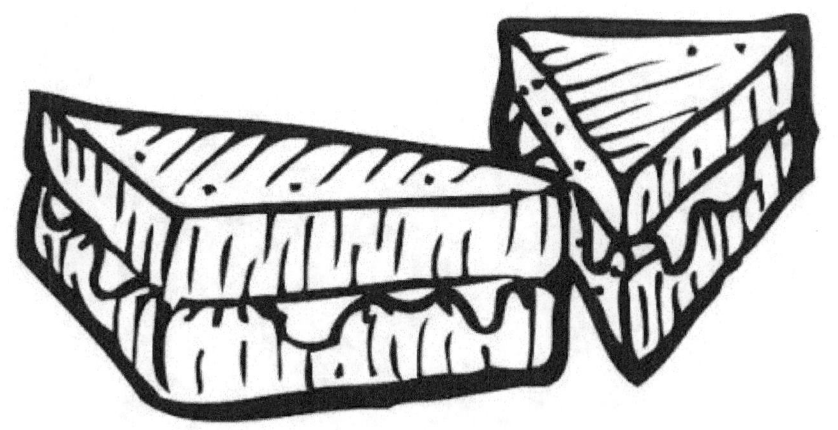